Gymn

Stretching

Build strength and flexibility
for powerful gymnastics

14 Peaks Inc

Table of Contents

Introduction

Flexibility is to a gymnast like swimming to a fish. Beautiful graceful gymnast display great flexibility and aesthetically pleasing lines. This purpose of this book is to focus on flexibility for those beautiful poses displayed in gymnastics. However, and this is key, with that flexibility must come strength. Gymnastics is about becoming strong with that flexibility.

There are several tools that can help with gymnastics flexibility and strength. A few of these are the Ballet Stretch Band, a Leg Stretcher (goes over the door) and a Gymnastics Strength Band. This book is a combination of the three. Choose from the different tools depending on your goals. These three tools are an indispensible component of a gymnasts' stretching regimen. Harnessing the power of elastic and static bands while being lightweight and portable, these tools are a great way to increase flexibility in a fun and dynamic way. The Ballet Stretch Band and the Leg Stretcher will work on passive flexibility while the Gymnastics Strength Band will work on flexibility and strength in active stretching.

In our book *Stretching Your Limits*, there are over 30 Ballet Stretch Band stretches, and in our book *Stretching Your Limits 2*, there are over 30 stretches for the Leg Stretcher. This book will cover those lightly but will mainly focus on the Gymnastics Strength Band, because in addition to gaining strength while stretching, one will gain flexibility.

While increasing flexibility, you will also want to strengthen the muscles responsible for holding the stretched limbs. This helps prevent injury and as a bonus makes your gymnastics more powerful. The Ballet Stretch Band and the Leg Stretcher come into play because passive stretching will be important on the off days. In fact, passive stretching can be done every day!

The intent of this book, strength gains while stretching, takes a unique combination of flexibility and strength. This is the beauty of combining workout equipment. One is not better. They can work in unison.

Chapter 1

Gymnastics Flexibility

While the Ballet Stretch Band and the Leg Stretcher are very powerful tools, we will start off with the the Gymnastics Strength Band. Our first two books focus on the Leg Stretcher, and the Ballet Stretch Band therefore we will only go over those briefly and if you need more details please refer to our first books in the series.

The Ballet Stretch Band and the Leg Stretcher can be purchased on Amazon.com and the Gymnastics Strength Band is a tool that can be made at home or purchased on Amazon. Using elastic as resistance, the Gymnastics Strength Band improves flexibility while simultaneously strengthening muscles. Balance is enhanced as well. There are many flexibility enhancers on the market that are great. However, this one is specifically for enhancing poses with power. It targets exact stretches that are utilized in gymnastics.

Being able to mimic the exact movements specific to gymnastics helps with muscle memory, making it easier to remember and execute the movements. If you watched the Olympic medalist Simone Biles on *Dancing with the Stars*, she stated this fact over and over. When asked how she did so well and how she remembered all the choreography, she would smile her big smile and answer, "muscle memory." The brain actually  creates new myelin sheaths allowing you to remember these moves for years to come.

Because the Gymnastics Strength Band uses elastic resistance similar to those who work out with strength bands, it also increases  muscle strength. Those strength gains are specific to the muscles you choose to utilize in the movements. As the band stretches, resistance increases, providing a stimulus to the muscle. This not only builds strength and flexibility, but proprioception as you balance. Many believe that strength is actually what makes you more flexible, and that makes this a dual threat.

Let's dive a little deeper into the strength portion as many believe this is what makes you more flexible. Training with elastic resistance provides a variable resistance throughout the stretch or exercise, eliminating the possibility of using momentum and cheating your way through the movement. Working against this resistance forces the muscle to respond with increased effort, which promotes the development of muscular growth, strength and power.

The Leg Stretcher on the other hand does not build strength, though it is great for building flexibility. You use your arms to pull your leg into certain positions.

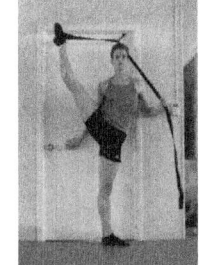

The Leg Stretcher uses passive stretching. The Gymnastics Strength Band is active stretching. They both have their place as you would not use the Gymnastics Strength Band, which is training strength, every day as your muscles would break down. However, you can do passive stretching daily, which is what the Leg Stretcher provides. Combined, they work great and can be an excellent addition to your gymnastics training routine.

The Gymnastics Stretch Band is growing in popularity, and it allows users to improve muscle tone by simulating movements that could be used in gymnastics routines. The product provides resistance, which increases the more it is stretched, meaning the muscles used are stimulated to improve their performance and strength.

What If I Am Already Flexible?

All three of these tools are great and the bonus is the Gymnastics Strength Band builds strength! The Gymnastics Strength Band not only allows you to stretch in functional dance positions, but it lets you strengthen while in the exact pose allowing the muscles to remember. The ultimate goal is not just gaining the flexibility required but gaining the strength necessary to sustain the movement.

Flexibility paired with strength is imperative for functional movements required in gymnastics. Utilizing the elastic resistance when performing stretches or exercises with the Gymnastics Strength Band increases muscle strength in a safe, productive manner.

Increasing Strength

As the band stretches, resistance increases, providing a stimulus to the muscle. This resistance does not rely on gravity. Instead, elastic resistance requires muscle activation throughout the muscle's range of motion, eliminating the possibility of using momentum and cheating your way through the exercise.

Moreover, strength training with elastic resistance provides variable resistance to promote the development of muscular strength and endurance. In a variable resistance exercise, the force applied to the muscle varies at each stage in order to create constant tension, causing the muscle to work harder to execute the movement. The result is a stronger, more controlled execution of functional movements necessary to be at the top of your game!

Chapter 2

The Basics

We stretch when we wake up and when we feel tired. Stretching helps to push blood into circulation, thus increasing the volume of blood pumped out with each heartbeat. This means more blood, more energy and more healing power to the muscles. Therefore, stretching can help you recover and stay healthy so that you can perform often and with less energy.

Stretching is the act of extending or lengthening the muscles and if you are stretching for flexibility you will increase how far the muscle can stretch. Stretching involves straightening or lengthening your complete structure to improve the muscles' elasticity.

The history of stretching can be traced as far back as the time of the ancient Greeks, who used stretching exercises as part of the training routine for their athletes and military personnel, as well as for general health maintenance.  Hippocrates and Galen, the two great contributors to the field of medicine, explored the therapeutic advantages of stretching. Stretching has been here since the beginning of time, just look at animals and how they stretch throughout the day.

Stretching is also therapeutic. In 1874, Dr. Andrew Taylor (US) introduced the science of osteopathy. Osteopathic treatment utilizes passive stretching of the soft tissues to restore normal structure and function. Later on, stretching found another therapeutic use when, in 1895, chiropractic was established, based on the hypothesis that every problem originates from misalignment of the vertebrae that restricts the flow of energy from the brain. Chiropractors rely on muscle manipulation as well as stretching.

Stretching is an important part of every warm-up as it prepares the muscles and gets the blood running to prime the body for impending action. *Dynamic* stretching is done before a workout and *passive* stretching after a workout. With age, if our physical activity level decreases, our joints stiffen and our muscles tighten. Regular stretching not only helps increase flexibility and range of motion but also improves posture and a sense of well-being. It just keeps us feeling good!

This book's focus is on stretching for gymnastics and those who need to be extremely flexible and strong. That said, anyone can do these stretches and benefit greatly. So, feel free to jump in there with your kids who are stretching.

The Physiology of Stretching

Before going into detail about the benefits of stretching, a little insight into the physiology of stretching is helpful.

As a muscle is stretched, the muscle fibers elongate. Once the muscle fibers elongate to their maximum limit, further stretching forces the collagen fibers in the surrounding connective tissue to align themselves along the line of force. This helps to realign the disorganized fibers and is the basis behind the rehabilitation of scar tissue.

When the muscle is stretched, stretch receptors, the specialized nerve endings present in the muscles and tendons, send signals to the brain initiating "the stretch reflex," which is a protective reflex to counter the increase in muscle length by causing it to contract. The more sudden the stretching, the stronger the stretch reflex will be. This reflex maintains muscle tone and reduces the risk of injury.

When the muscle is held in a stretched position for a long time, the nerves get accustomed to the new length and this diminishes the stretch reflex, allowing for greater lengthening of the muscle.

Strength and Flexibility

Strength training and flexibility training should go hand in hand. It is a common misconception that there must always be a trade-off between flexibility and strength. Obviously, if you neglect flexibility training altogether in order to train for strength, you sacrifice flexibility. The truth is, flexibility training and strength training can enhance one another.

Overflexibility

As you get "looser" or more limber in a particular joint, less support is given to the joint by its surrounding muscles. Excessive flexibility can be just as bad as not enough, because both increase your risk of injury. The beauty of the Gymnastics Strength Band is that it increases your strength in tandom with flexibility.

Once a muscle has reached its absolute maximum length, attempting to stretch the muscle further only serves to stretch the ligaments and put undue stress upon the tendons. Ligaments will tear when stretched to more than 6% of their normal length. Tendons do not naturally lengthen. Even when stretched ligaments and tendons do not tear, loose joints or a decrease in the joint's stability can occur, vastly increasing the risk of injury.

Chapter 3

Types of Flexiblity

There are different types of stretching, but both fall under two categories. Stretches are either dynamic (meaning they involve motion) or static (meaning they involve no motion). Dynamic stretches affect dynamic flexibility and static stretches affect static flexibility.

The different types of stretching are:

1. Ballistic stretching

2. Dynamic stretching

3. Active stretching

4. Passive (or relaxed) stretching

5. Static stretching

6. Isometric stretching

Stretches are numerous and come to the human being sometimes naturally turning into something beautiful and artistic. Stretching helps the body accommodate some of the strenuous routines that come with gymnastics, as well as help recover.

Current researchers advise athletes to start with active stretches because these warm the muscles and get them ready to sustain exercise. These are called dynamic stretches. According to the acclaimed philosopher of the nervous system, Sir Charles Sherrington, there are two classes of muscles: the agonist muscles, which contract, and the antagonist muscles, which inhibit. Through active stretching routines, the individual can increase flexibility, not to the point of pain but just as far as the body elasticity permits.

Some stretches are slow and gentle and passive stretching is one of those. It is the type of stretching that targets a particular muscle group in a controlled way. This form involves the individual being relaxed and not holding any particular form of motion while the trained professional does the job. There are several exercises that alleviate pain and malaise in different muscles and this range of motion is important to increase soft tissue flexibility and functionality of the specific body part, to avert and/or improve contractures in the body part, to enhance healing and to reduce pain. If you have seen a soccer player grab his leg during overtime with a cramp, you most likely saw a trainer doing static stretching on the calf by pushing the foot back.

Equipment, such as the Ballet Stretch Bands and the Flexiblity Strap, use a lot of passive stretching. Letting your body hang over your toes while relaxing and without pushing is an example of passive stretching.

The ballistic stretch involves rapidly bouncing a part of the body. The swift recoil from one angle, to and fro or from side to side, is what many of us grew up doing whenever our coaches told us to stretch. It is however a dangerous stretch. It can tear muscles and is no longer recommended. We mention it here only to say don't do it!

Most athletes like to do a stretch called the sit and reach, where they sit down on the floor, extend their legs, and reach their arms out to touch their toes. Most trainers and coaches require their athletes to do this stretch before any sort of practice, sport, or game. However, this type of stretch is not to be utilized before a workout. This is static stretching and should be used after a workout, not before. Dynamic stretching, instead of static stretching, should always be done before exercising.

Dynamic stretching is great in warmups before workouts. The dynamic stretch enables one to be warm muscles. It is movement that becomes really effective when synced to potential workout routines. Rolling out your arms and hip are examples of dynamic stretches. Dynamic stretches are numerous and can be achieved through the different parts of the body.

Another example of a dynamic stretch is swinging the leg back and forth such as a leg lift. One dynamic stretch starts with standing straight, then moving the leg out to the side in a side leg lift. The movement is controlled and fluid.

Another example that is especially helpful for the neck and the waist is called "rolling out the neck" or "rolling out the waist." Repeating at intervals, this stretch yields great results and the more you do these kinds of movements, the more relaxed you become.

Isometric stretches fall in the class of static stretching since there is little motion applied to muscle contractions. This does not mean isometric stretching is just static stretching; it goes beyond stretching by actually activating the muscles for some strength gains.

Some specialists fault static stretching for not encouraging muscles to become elastic because of the stillness the concept entails. Isometric stretches enable the muscles to remember through signals directed at the muscle fibers; therefore, isometric stretches are more robust and effective than their static relatives.

One efficient way of performing an isometric stretch is by sitting on a mat with your legs in front and hands holding the tips of your toes. From this position flex muscles by contracting them and putting pressure on them. This should be done for about twenty seconds.

Static stretching is very popular and it is essentially the ability to hold a muscle in place. This is most likely what you think of when you picture an athlete stretching before a performance, but science now shows it is best to perform dynamic stretching after a performance or a workout.

This can involve the hamstring, the quads, and the stomach. Most professional athletes do static stretches before performing in order to augment performance and avoid injury. Yet, this stretch has seen some controversy as recent research shows that static stretches impede the body's reflex to spring and recoil through the constant motion of holding still.

Research also claims that static stretches actually make the body more liable to injury because there is a lack of balance in the movement. Because of this, static stretches should be done at the end of your workout routine. This is where you are going to get the most gains in flexibility.

Before composing a particular stretching routine, you must first decide which types of flexibility you wish to increase and which stretching methods are best for achieving them. The best way to increase dynamic flexibility is by performing dynamic stretches, supplemented with static stretches after the workout.

Overall, you should expect to increase flexibility gradually. We recommend taking it slow and advancing as you feel comfortable. Stretching should not hurt.

Chapter 4

Stretching the Benefits

- *Enhanced Range of Joint Movement*

  Stretching opens up your joints and improves their range of motion. This increases your mobility and helps to maintain the balance of the body.

- *Improved Body Flexibility*

  This can be achieved by properly warming up before starting your routine.

- *Greater Power to Execute Certain Movements and Skills*

When you do a wide selection of activities, your body will be in better shape and you'll be able to accomplish more things. You can jump higher without soreness whenever you land.

- *Reduced Risk of Injury*

  Warmup exercises help to prepare your body for an upcoming event. Instead of jerking into motion, stretching increases the momentum in a controlled fashion.

- *Damage Prevention*

  A person can avoid damage to joints, tendons and muscle tissue with stretching. When the muscular tissues and tendons are well-flexed, they are considered to be in excellent working condition. This may help make your recovery more rapid and help decrease soreness of other parts of the body. The muscles in the body will manage to take more exhausting and rigorous actions while being less likely to be injured.

- *Improved Circulation*

  Stretching improves circulation to the muscles. Blood carries oxygen to the muscles, reduces the build-up of waste that leads to muscle fatigue and has healing power to repair damaged tissue. More blood to the tissues means improved performance and rapid healing.

- *Better Posture*

  Tense muscles affect posture, leading to aches and pains. Poor posture also disturbs the normal functioning of the internal organs. Regular stretching prevents stiffness and tightening of the muscles and helps to keep the torso well aligned.

- *Increase Power*

  Stretching more will also give your body more power when done with strength in mind.

- *Body Awareness*

  Increasing your amount of stretching will enhance your awareness of what your body is capable of doing.

- *Never Stretch Cold*

  Sretching cold makes you more susetible to injury. Whenyou stretch cold, the muscles are tight and tense and more likely to suffer from a tear or sprain. A light warmup of at least five minutes is needed to get your body prepared for stretching. Often, it is ideal to do this right after your workout is completed. If you are stretching on a non-workout day, a light warmup beforehand can help get your body prepared. This could include jogging at a slow pace, jumping jacks, skipping or walking at a brisk pace.

- *Ease into the Stretch*

  Next, make sure you ease into your stretch. As you go about your stretching routine, do not rush by jerking your muscle into position. Quickly forcing the muscle will only increase your risk factor of an injury. Go slow. Breathe as you lower yourself down and pause when it becomes uncomfortable. Take another deep breath in, pause again and move lower into the stretch.

Chapter 5

Tips for the Gymnastics Strength Band

Before we get to the actual stretching, here are a few tips.

- *Right Length*

  Make sure the Gymnastics Stretch Band is at the right length before exercise making sure they are equal at all times.

- *Shorter Straps*

  The exercise will be made more difficult by shortening the straps, so if you want to increase the resistance to increase the intensity of the exercise, this is the step that you will need to take.

- *Ankle Injuries*

  When using the Gymnastics Strength Band, you should never use it around your ankle. Instead, make sure it is placed around the middle of your foot to avoid injuring your ankle.

- *Neck Injuries*

While you're using the Gymnastics Strength Band, never place it around your neck at any time, as the pressure could cause injury.

Keep in mind that your body is like a perfect machine; however, you should know your limits and listen to your body.

Now you have the facts you need to know regarding your stretching routine. Don't overlook this critical element of your workout program. Let's get to it!

Chapter 6

The Warm-Ups

Warming up is cool. The reason it's cool is because getting hurt is not. By now, you understand that a couple of static stretches are not going to carry you through your performance. A leg up once or twice won't get you through your event. It is serious and is worth doing right.

Arm Rolls Outs Aka Swimmers

Rolling your arms out gets your body warmed up. It gets your blood pumping and fuels your muscles.

1. Stand tall with your arms to your side.

2. Bring your arms up the sky

3. Roll forward ten times and then backward ten times, like you are doing front crawl in the pool.

4. Repeat ten times.

Jumping Jacks

Let's get that blood pumping! Jumping jacks are a fantastic way to raise your core temperature, which gets everything moving and warmed up:

1. Stand with your feet close together, arms to your sides.

2. Tighten your abdominal muscles so your pelvis is forward and your lower back is straight.

3. Slightly bend your knees.

4. Now, jump so you land with your feet a bit over shoulder-width apart.

5. At the same time, raise your arms above your head. (You should be on the balls of your feet.)

6. With your knees slightly bent, jump again, as you bring your feet together and your arms back to your sides.

7. Repeat fifteen times.

Neck and Shoulder Roll

Your neck is used widely in many sports and activities. Be sure to warm it up well with an exercise like this one.

1. Stand straight and tall with your feet shoulder-width apart.

2. Slowly tilt your head to the side. Gently pull.

3. Repeat on the other side.

Jogging in Place

This is a very simple warm up, but one that is priceless.

1. Hold your arms to your side.

2. Breathe deep and slow.

3. Jog gently in place for ten steps on each foot.

4. Gradually pump up the pace ten more steps.

5. Go one more round, even faster.

6. Gradually cool down your pace.

7. Complete with your arms beside you in a stance position.

Rolling It Back and Rolling It Up

This exercise will help your body establish balance and mobility in the neck, back, spine, and hamstrings. It will warm up your abdominal muscles, get your blood circulating, relieve tension, help create space between the vertebrae, and promote proper posture as well.

1. Drop your chin to your chest.

2. Roll through your back reaching your hands to the floor.

3. When you feel the need, bend your knees.

4. Stretch and hold.

5. Slowly, go all the way back up to a standing position.

6. Repeat five to ten times.

Don't stay down and hold it or you will turn this into a static stretch. Keep it rolling slowly.

Take Time for the Spine

The health of your spine is crucial, not just in the performing arts and in sports, but for your life in general. The spine is the second most injured body part in dancers, preceded only by leg injuries. It is a leading injury in gymnasts.

Spinal injuries can lead to chronic pain. Here's a warm-up to help make sure your spine is prepared.

1. Kneel on the floor on your hands and knees with your palms directly under your shoulders and your knees under your hip bones. Your fingers will be pointed away from you.

2. Tuck in your chin, and then curve your back upward toward the ceiling. Gently pull.

3. Arch your back, pulling your head up toward the ceiling.

4. Tilt your tailbone up.

5. Return to your original position and repeat five times.

Hip Warm-Ups

Warm-ups are hip, literally. The hip is another part of the body widely used in ballet, dance, gymnastics, and most any other performing art or sport. You will need a lot of hip flexibility.

Did you know a turnout, the classic ballet starting position with toes and knees turned out and heels together, requires the work of six muscles located deep within your pelvic and hip area?

The hips are often overworked in many of the performing arts and in sports, as well. Make sure to warm them up each and every time.

1. Lay down on your back.

2. Pull your right knee to your chest.

3. Circle your bent leg out to the side.

4. Return your leg next to your other leg, lengthwise.

5. Repeat ten times.

6. Switch and do the same using your left leg.

Ankle Rotation Sensation

It goes without saying that your ankles need to be warmed up. Just think of how much weight is put on them just by walking. It is very important to get them ready to roll or not to roll.

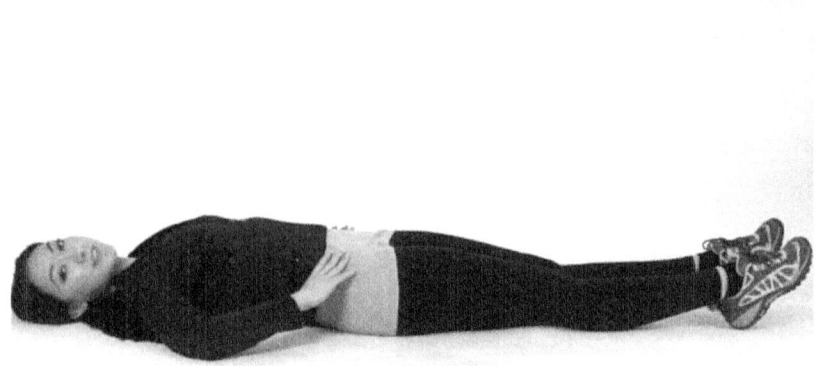

1. Lay on the floor.

2. Gently point the toe of your right foot.

3. Lift your right leg slightly off the floor.

4. Rotate your ankle in a circle.

5. Repeat ten times to the right and ten times to the left.

6. Now, do the same on your left side.

Tip: This exercise can also be done stranding. Sometimes students are asked to write their name with the foot to make it more fun.

Back Legs and Hips Dip

We've talked about how important it is to warm up the hips, but the hamstrings (back of the legs) are super significant too.

1. With your legs wide apart and your feet pointed out, bend your knees.

2. Drop your hips down to the floor to a deep, wide squat.

3. From there, bring one leg out straight to the side as you stretch.

4. Hold for twenty seconds.

5. Do both sides five times.

Chapter 7

Step-By-Step Instructions for your Gymnastics Strength Band

Arabesque with Chair Arm Extended

Make sure you keep your shoulders square and think of closing your ribs as you engage your abdominals; making this an active stretch.

1. To begin the arabesque, make sure you are holding on to something stable, and place both loops around your left foot.

2. Bend your left knee and draw it behind your back, such as when you do a quad stretch.

3. Put the strap over your right shoulder.

4. Extend the left leg into an arabesque, while continuing to hold the chair.

5. Now, extend your right arm.

Arabesque 2

1. To begin the arabesque, make sure you are holding on to something stable, then, place both loops around your left foot.

2. Bend your left knee and draw it behind your back, like a quad stretch.

3. Thread your right arm through the straps, placing the foam pad around your right shoulder.

4. Extend the left leg into an arabesque.

5. Gently let go of the chair as you balance.

Arabesque 3

1. To begin the arabesque, make sure you are holding on to something stable, and place both loops around your left foot.

2. Bend your left knee and draw it behind your back, much like a quad stretch.

3. Thread your right arm through the straps, placing the foam pad around your right shoulder.

4. Extend the left leg into an arabesque.

5. Slowly let go of the chair and extend your arm.

Rear Leg Stretch

1. To begin the arabesque, make sure you are holding on to something stable, and place both loops around your left foot.

2. Bend your left knee and draw it behind your back, much like a quad stretch.

3. Thread your right arm through the straps, placing the foam pad around your right shoulder.

4. Extend the left leg into an arabesque.

   5. Use the chair to support yourself as you lean forward, working on the strength and stretching of the legs.

Standing Front Split

1. Set up this stretch as you did the arabesque.

2. Keeping the Gymnastics Stretch Band in the same position as the arabesque stretch; bring your body down towards the ground, while holding onto a chair.

3. As your body nears the base of the chair, your working leg will extend farther.

Advanced Front Split

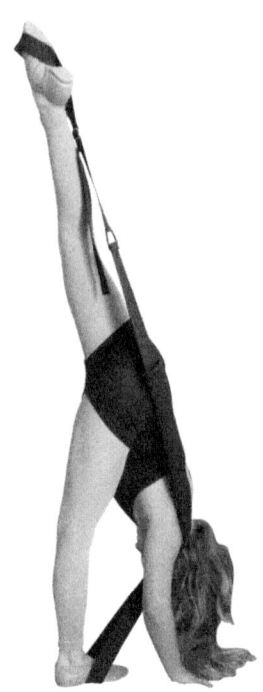

1. Keeping the Gymnastics Stretch Band in the same position as the arabesque stretch, bring your body down towards the ground.

2. As your body nears the floor, your working leg will extend.

3. Make sure you are balanced evenly as you slowly lower yourself to the ground.

4. Another option is to start with your hands on the ground and slowly extend the leg.

Side Split

1. Lay on your side with shoulders squared.

2. Put Gymnastics Strength Band around your right foot.

3. Slowly extend your leg until it is fully extended.

4. Gently pull down to gain a greater stretch and to work on strength.

Side Extensions

1. Hold on to something stable.

2. Place loops over your right foot.

3. Wrap the padded area of the Gymnastics Strength Band over your opposite shoulder, and make sure the straps pass behind your neck!

4. Slowly extend the leg until it is straight.

Middle Splits

1. Place Gymnastics Strength Band's loops over both of your feet

2. With bent legs, wrap the padding of the Gymnastics Stretch Band behind your neck or upper back.

3. Slowly extend your legs into the splits.

4. You can do this stretch with pointed or flexed feet.

5. Make sure to engage your quads to stabilize your knees, and use your abdominals to maintain your balance.

Middle Splits Laying Down

1. Lay on your back with your shoulders flat.

2. Place Gymnastics Strength Band's loops over both of your feet as pictured above.

3. With bent legs, wrap the padding of the Gymnastics Stretch Band behind your neck or upper back.

4. Slowly extend your legs into the splits.

5. You can do this stretch with pointed or flexed feet.

Wheel Pose

1. Loop the Gymnastics Strength Band around each forearm with the center of the Gymnastics Strength Band around your shins.

2. Actively push the shins into the center of the strap.

3. Keep your feet parallel and facing the front of the mat; also keep your hands parallel.

Single-Legged Wheel Variation

1. Try this challenging single-legged wheel pose! The setup is the same as the Wheel Pose except the strap will only go around one shin.

2. From here, practice lifting the leg up towards the ceiling and holding for 5 full breaths.

3. Repeat on opposite side.

Gymnastics Stretch Band Pigeon Pose & Variations

1. With a bent back leg, put both loops around the right foot.

2. Put the foam part of Gymnastics Strength Band around the left shoulder.

3. Hold this pose to build strength and stretch the groin.

The Gymnastics Strength Band Assists in Binded Cow Face Pose

1. Start in a seated position, bringing a bent knee to a 90-degree angle and placing the other bent leg on top of it. Each ankle should be in line with the opposite knee.

2. To assist in the holding, hold onto the elastic part of the Gymnastics Stretch Band.

3. Start with it in your top hand and bring the Gymnastics Strength Band to the rotated arm on the bottom. You can gently pull on the elastic band to engage through the tops of the arms.

Lower Back Release with the Gymnastics Strength Band

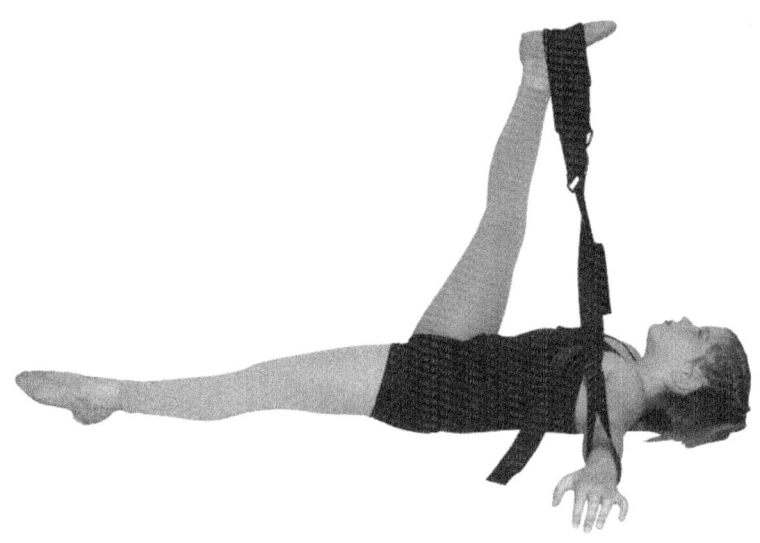

Try this pose with your Gymnastics Stretch Band for a deep hamstring stretch.

1. Put your arms in each of the straps.

2. Place one leg in the padded portion of Gymnastics Strength Band.

3. Slowly extend the leg.

Forward Pose Variation

1. Put one loop around each foot and place the padded portion around your back.

2. Begin with feet hip-width distance apart and release the body in a forward fold. For tighter hamstrings, keep the knees bent slightly.

3. It's more important to have a lengthened spine than straight legs.

Variation 1: With the Gymnastics Stretch Band on the lower back, gently try to touch your toes.

Variation 2: You can reverse this stretch by placing Gymnastics Strength Band padding under the feet and one loop in each hand. This is more of an active stretch, as you bring the torso closer to the body. Try both variations and see what works best for your body!

Low Lunge with the Gymnastics Stretch Band

1. Place the center of the Gymnastics Strength Band under the back shin and take the loops in your hands.

2. Press your hips forward as you press the straps up towards the sky, finding a full spinal extension.

3. Focus on pressing up into the straps.

Gymnastics Strength Band Monster Walks

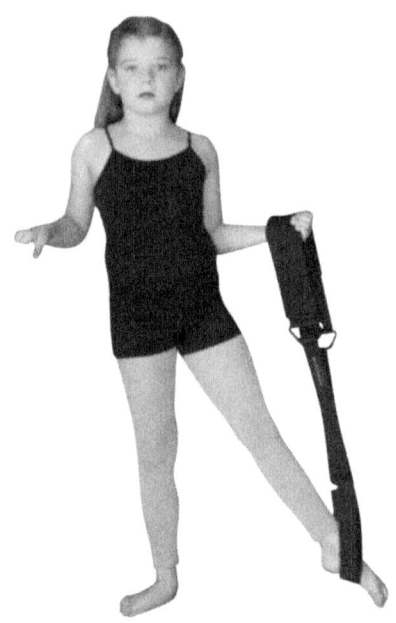

1. Place Gymnastics Strength Band on the left foot.

2. Hold Gymnastics Strength Band in your left hand.

3. Walk sideways, keeping your pressure on the left leg by pulling gently with the left hand.

4. This helps strengthen the inside of the leg.

5. Walk sideways 15 steps, then switch to the other leg.

Gymnastics Strength Band Hamstring Stretch

1. Place Gymnastics Strength Band around the feet.

2. Hold the other end with your hands.

3. Gently pull down, stretching the back of the legs.

Hamstring Stretch One Leg

1. Place the Gymnastics Strength Band around the feet.

2. Hold the other end with your hands.

3. Gently pull down, stretching the back of the legs.

4. Lift one leg off the floor gently.

5. Hold for 15 seconds and switch legs.

Runner's Stretch

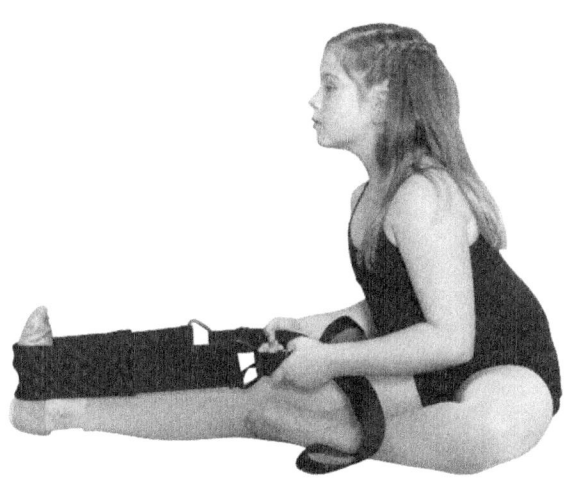

1. Place Gymnastics Strength Band around the right foot.

2. Hold the other end with your hands.

3. Put your left leg in a runner's pose.

4. Gently pull down, stretching the back of the legs.

5. Lift one leg off the floor gently.

6. Hold for 15 seconds and, then, switch legs.

Gymnastics Strength Band Yoga: Dancer's Pose

1. Put Gymnastics Strength Band's padded end around the left flexed foot (top of the foot).

2. Hold Gymnastics Strength Band's loops in both hands.

3. Gently pull the left leg up.

Front Split

1. Place Gymnastics Strength Band over the left foot with the leg bent.

2. Place the other end on the right sholder.

3. Slowly extend the right leg into the front splits.

4. Make sure to keep the tension in Gymnastics Strength Band for the duration of the exercise by pressing the back foot actively into the strap and pulling back the opposite shoulder.

Quadricep Stretch

1. Place Gymnastics Strength Band on the left foot.

2. Put Gymnastics Strength Band over the right shoulder.

3. Gently pull with the right hand stretching the quadricep.

Bonus Chapter 8

Optimize Your Workout with a Leg Stretcher

Stretching maximizes your workout so you can get to the top of your game. When you stretch using a leg stretcher, the benefits are magnified even more. With regular use of your leg stretcher, you'll be at your peak performance in no time!

What Is a Leg Stretcher?

A leg stretcher is a device that is used to help you stretch and strengthen your leg and lower back muscles. Generally, it has a bracket to attach to the top of a door frame, a pulley and pull cord and a sling. You simple insert your leg into the sling then raise and lower it in order to target a particular muscle or muscle group.

In order to optimize your stretching routine, you can use a leg-stretching device that will help you stretch properly and effectively.

Practically anyone can use a leg stretcher. As long as you have enough space to move around a little and a door, ceiling or wall to attach it to and have no serious physical condition that would put you at risk, it should work great for you.

Some of the people who use a leg stretcher are:

- Ballerinas

- Dancers

- Gymnasts

- Runners

- Martial Artist

- Swimmers

- Ice Skaters

- Sprinters

- Climbers

But, leg stretching devices aren't just for hard core athletic people. They also work wonders for anyone wishing to:

- Perform a physical activity.

- Promote good balance.

- Promote good posture.

- Limber up muscles and increase range of motion.

- Loosen up muscles to relieve pain.

- Destress

- Prevent injuries caused by stiff muscles and tight joints.

What Can a Leg Stretcher Do for Me?

If you want to take your stretching to the next level, a leg stretcher can certainly help. Stretching is more comfortable and more productive when using the device. It will help you balance and adds resistance so you can reach your stretching goals easier and faster.

One of the best kept secrets is that a leg-stretching machine can make you have a better appearance too. The next time you are in a crowd, note the difference in the way people carry themselves and what it says for their overall looks. Those with good posture and great balance just seem to glide around the room with ease and confidence. A good stretching routine can help you achieve that air as well.

Types of Leg Stretchers

Leg stretchers are different from leg-stretching machines although, for the most part, they are used for the same goal: to help you stretch. Machines are larger, heavier and take up much more space. They are usually found in gyms or in homes where there is a designated workout room and generally cost a lot more than a leg stretcher.

Leg stretchers attach to a door, a wall or the ceiling. They are portable, inexpensive and are a cinch to use. They basically accomplish the same thing as the machine does…they maximize your stretching.

There are many different styles of leg stretchers and various levels of cost as well. Be sure to get one that is well made. Be sure to check out the quality of any stretcher you are considering. Look for package deals as well. Often times you can get one with extras, like a carry bag or additional features, for the same price.

What Kind of Exercises Can I Do with a Leg Stretcher?

Stretches done with the help of a leg stretcher are considered to be static. There are many variances of stretches that can be done with the device so that you can flex different muscles and muscle groups. You'll find plenty of great stretch exercises in this book and you can add in some of your own customizations if you'd like as well.

Setting Up Your Leg Stretcher

Over the Door Type

1. Place the smaller strap over the door.

2. Close the door securely.

3. Place the longer strap through the "D ring" and pull it through.

4. Pull the straps to desired length.

5. Check to be sure the device is firmly in place and all parts are working properly.

6. Secure your foot in the loop and begin your stretches.

Ceiling or Wall

1. Drill a hole in the ceiling or wall.

2. Get a heavy-duty bolt type hook (make sure it is strong enough).

3. Screw the hook in securely.

4. Hook shorter strap with "D ring."

5. Pull longer strap through "D ring."

6. Pull straps to desired length.

7. Check to make sure the device is firmly in place and that all parts of the unit are properly working.

8. Secure your foot in the loop and begin your stretches.

Devices with Cables and Pulleys

Some leg stretchers come with cables or pulleys. Instructions vary but should be included in the packaging. Many even have video instructions, which make the assembly even easier.

Cautions and Concerns

Here are some pointers that can help keep you safe while stretching:

- Always be sure to check with your physician before starting any exercise regime.

- Don't skimp when purchasing your stretching unit.

- Read the instructions that come with your leg stretcher.

- Never push your body past the first inkling of pain and tightness. Work up gradually.

- If you are sick or injured, take a break from serious stretching.

- Keep hydrated.

- Wear appropriate clothing that won't get tangled up in the device.

- If you suspect the door, ceiling or wall you have your leg stretcher attached to is becoming weak, have it checked out before using the device any more.

- Be sure to lock the door you are using so no one can open it and cause you to get hurt.

Bonus Chapter 9

Step-by-Step Stretch Band Instructions

STRETCHES FROM THE BUTTERFLY POSITION

Butterfly Stretch

1. Sit on the floor in the butterfly position with your back straight and shoulders down
2. Loop one end of the stretch band around the center of your right foot. Bring the band behind your back where it falls above your hips.
3. Loop the left end of the band around the center of your left foot. Gently pull your heels toward you.
4. Use your elbows to push your legs toward the floor.
5. Breathe deep and hold the pose for twenty to thirty seconds while concentrating on your breathing and the muscles you are stretching.
6. Relax for ten to twenty seconds. Repeat two times.

Side Stretch

1. Sit on the floor in the butterfly position with your back straight.
2. Place the band around your waist and loop it around each foot.
3. Bend your knees and let them fall to the ground. Hold your left arm above your head and stretch your side with your right palm placed on the floor behind your right knee.
4. Hold the pose for twenty to thirty seconds while concentrating on your breathing and the muscles you are stretching.
5. Relax for twenty seconds. Repeat two times.

Side Hamstring Stretch

1. From the butterfly position, slowly stretch your left leg out to the side, where it is even with your left hip. Keep your knee straight and your toes pointed up. Your right knee will be bent into your body.

2. With your back straight and your shoulders aligned forward, allow the band to pull your leg gently off the floor and hold.

3. Breathe deep. Hold the pose for twenty to thirty seconds while concentrating on your breathing and the muscles you are stretching.

4. Relax for ten to twenty seconds. Repeat two times.

Side Hamstring Stretch with Bend

1. From the side hamstring stretch position, place the palms of your hands on the floor on either side of your left leg, just below your knee.

2. Slowly allow your foot to be pulled up by the band.

3. Hold the pose for twenty to thirty seconds while concentrating on your breathing and the muscles you are stretching.

4. Relax for twenty seconds. Repeat two times.

Hamstring and Side Stretch

1. From the side hamstring stretch position, stretch your right side by stretching your right arm and hand up and over toward your left leg.

2. Hold the pose for twenty to thirty seconds while concentrating on your breathing and the muscles you are stretching.

3. Relax for twenty seconds. Repeat two times.

Hamstring and Back Stretch

1. From the side hamstring stretch position, slightly turn and look to your right side with your head turned to the right and the back side of your right hand touching your lower back.

2. Gently lift your left foot up while holding the top of your foot with your left hand.

3. Hold the pose for twenty to thirty seconds while concentrating on your breathing and the muscles you are stretching.

4. Relax for twenty seconds. Repeat two times.

Calf Stretch with Foot Hold

1. From the side hamstring stretch position, rest your right hand on your right knee while facing your left leg. Bend your right leg as far as possible, bracing it against the straight left leg.

2. Gently lift your foot up, holding the top of it with your left hand.

3. Hold for twenty to thirty seconds while concentrating on the muscles your stretching

4. Relax for twenty seconds. Repeat two times.

5. Repeat on the opposite side.

Calf Stretch Sitting Tall with a Band

1. Sit on the floor.

2. Loop one end of the band around your right foot.

3. Bend your right knee and place the sole of your right foot on your inner thigh.

4. Wrap the band around your waist in the back and extend it to where it is looped around your left foot.

5. Flex your left foot toward you while holding the band with your right hand above your left knee.

6. Place your left hand on your lower hip.

7. Slightly lift the band up so your lower calf and foot are off the ground. You should feel a slight stretch.

8. Hold for ten seconds.

9. Repeat two times.

10. Switch sides and repeat.

Calf Stretch Using Band

1. From the side hamstring stretch position take hold of the loop on your left foot and gently pull your body toward your knee.

2. Hold the pose for twenty to thirty seconds while concentrating on your breathing and the muscles you are stretching.

3. Relax for seconds. Repeat two times.

4. Switch and repeat on the opposite side.

Middle Splits

1. The middle split, is the ultimate in stretching. Sit on the floor with your back straight and your shoulders aligned.

2. Attach the band to your right foot and get in the side hamstring stretch position.

3. Gently stretch your left legs into the middle split position, as pictured, and place your palms on the floor directly in front of you. Hold the pose for twenty to thirty seconds while concentrating on your breathing and the muscles you are stretching.

4. Relax for twenty seconds. Repeat two times.

Lying Forward in Middle Splits

1. This stretch takes the middle splits to the limit. After you have completed the middle split exercise above, lean forward with your chest touching the floor in front of you.

2. Bend your elbows and place your hands under your chin. Hold for twenty to thirty seconds while someone snaps your picture!

3. Relax for twenty seconds. Repeat two times.

FRONT SPLIT STRETCHES

Half Front Split

1. Start in the butterfly position but put the strap on your right shoulder instead of your right foot. Place the other end on the left foot.

2. Slowly extend your left leg backward into a half split.

3. Stretch your left leg out behind you with a slight bend of your knee. Hold your left arm up above your head.

4. Hold the pose for twenty to thirty seconds while concentrating on your breathing and the muscles you are stretching.

5. Relax for twenty seconds. Repeat two times.

6. Switch and repeat on the opposite side.

Half Splits with Quadriceps Stretch

1. Sit on the floor and double loop the band around your left foot, then loop it once around your right upper foot and position it so it goes over your shoulder from one foot to the other.

2. As you assume the front split position, bend your left leg and raise your foot up and slightly to the right.

3. Stretch your right leg up slightly off the floor. Place your palms on the floor on either side of your upper left leg.

4. Hold the pose for twenty to thirty seconds while concentrating on your breathing and the muscles you are stretching.

5. Relax for twenty seconds. Repeat two times.

6. Switch and repeat on the opposite side.

Half Splits Strength Work

1. Sit on the floor and loop the band around your left foot once. Slowly bring it over your shoulder and loop around your right upper foot. Position it so it goes over your shoulder from one foot to the other.

2. As you assume the front split position, bend your left leg. It will raise slightly. You can work on strength by trying to push it down into a full front split or hold it for flexibility in the front split position.

3. Place your palms on the floor on either side of your upper left leg.

4. Hold the pose for twenty to thirty seconds while concentrating on your breathing and the muscles you are stretching.

5. Relax for twenty seconds. Repeat two times.

6. Switch and repeat on the opposite side.

Front Splits

1. Start in the butterfly position, but put the strap on your right shoulder and on your left foot.

2. Slowly, extend your left leg backward into a half splits.

3. Slowly, extend your front leg into the full front splits.

4. Place your palms on the floor on either side of your right outstretched leg.

5. Point your toes and hold for twenty to thirty seconds while concentrating on your breathing and the muscles you are stretching.

6. Relax for twenty seconds. Repeat two times.

7. Switch and repeat on the opposite side.

LUNGE EXERCISES

Kneeling Quadriceps Stretch

1. Stand with your legs a hip-width apart.

2. Loop the band around the middle of your left foot, and then bring it over your right shoulder.

3. Step forward with your right leg and plant your left knee on the floor so it is bent and your right foot is on the ground.

4. With your left hand on the floor, lower your body to where your front left thigh is parallel to the floor. At this point, the stretch band should be snug.

5. Hold for twenty to thirty seconds while concentrating on your breathing and the muscles you are stretching.

6. Relax twenty seconds. Repeat two times.

7. Switch and repeat on the opposite side.

Arms Overhead Quadriceps Stretch

1. This is another lunge that will stretch your hamstrings as well as your back, shoulders, and arms. Perform the kneeling quadriceps stretch then step forward with your left leg.

2. Hold the band with both hands and stretch with arms extended above your head with your back straight, stretching upward.

3. Hold the pose for twenty to thirty seconds while concentrating on your breathing and the muscles you are stretching.

4. Relax for twenty seconds. Repeat two times.

5. Switch and repeat on the opposite side.

STANDS WITH THE BAND

Holding Leg Lift

1. Stand facing the back of a chair and place your right hand on it. Loop the middle of the stretch band around your left leg. It should twist around your left knee and attach to your left foot. The other end will loop around your right shoulder.

2. Extend your left leg out to a ninety-degree angle while keeping your right hand on the chair and your left arm out in front of you.

3. Hold for twenty to thirty seconds while concentrating on your breathing and the muscles you are stretching.

4. Relax for twenty seconds. Repeat two times.

5. Switch and repeat on the opposite side.

Standing Front Split

This stretch is great to flex out your inner and outer thighs. It's also fantastic for your shoulders, arms, and back and helps your balance, as well.

1. Stand straight facing a chair.

2. Hold the band with your right hand, wrapping it around your wrist once.

3. Take the other end of the band over your right shoulder and loop it around your left foot.

4. Hold onto the chair with your left hand.

5. Lean forward toward the chair, slightly arching your back.

6. As you are leaning in, bring your left foot up over your head so you are basically doing the split in the air.

7. Slowly lower your left foot back to the ground while bringing your torso back to a standing position.

8. Hold for twenty to thirty seconds while concentrating on your breathing and the muscles you are stretching.

9. Repeat two times.

10. Switch sides and repeat.

Lord of the Dance Stretch

1. Wrap the band around your left foot. Stand on your right leg.

2. Hold the ends of the band with your hands held above your head and back a bit with your back arched slightly.

3. Lift your right leg up applying tension to the band. Your knee will be slightly bent and your foot will point toward the ceiling.

4. Hold for twenty to thirty seconds while concentrating on your breathing and the muscles you are stretching.

5. Return your left foot to the ground.

6. Repeat two times.

7. Work the other side.

Forward Facing Front Split

1. Stand with your right side facing a chair.

2. Hold on to the chair with your left hand with your elbow bent, arm crossing your upper abdomen.

3. Double loop your band around your right hand and your left foot.

4. Bring your right hand to the top of your head so your left foot is even with your head and the tension can be felt from the band.

5. Your right foot should remain on the ground.

6. Hold for ten seconds, while relaxing and concentrating on the muscles you are stretching.

7. Release and repeat two times.

8. Repeat on the opposite side.

Holding Leg Lift Floor Touch

1. Stand facing the back of the chair. Double the band over your left foot and hold it with your right fist.

2. Keep your right foot on the floor and your right leg straight while lifting your left leg up, bending it at the knee.

3. Hold the chair with your left hand while pressing your right hand with the band downward.

4. Hold the pose for twenty to thirty seconds while concentrating on your breathing and the muscles you are stretching.

5. Relax for twenty seconds. Repeat two times.

6. Repeat on the opposite side.

Standing Front Split

1. Stand with your left side facing a chair.

2. Hold on to the chair with your left arm. Slightly bend your arm at the elbow and hold the chair with your left hand.

3. Loop the band around your right hand and around your left foot.

4. Raise your right hand up beside your head with your elbow bent.

5. Pull your leg up over your head with your feet pointed.

6. Hold for thirty seconds, while relaxing and concentrating on the muscles being stretched.

7. Repeat two times.

8. Repeat on the opposite side.

Ballerina Pose

1. Loop the band around your right shoulder.

2. Bring the band across your shoulder, down your back and loop it around your left foot.

3. Hold your right arm out and your left arm forward and up as you bring your left foot back with a steady, slow motion.

4. Hold for ten seconds. Relax and concentrate on the muscles you are stretching.

5. Repeat two times.

6. Work on the opposite side.

En Pointe with Stretch Bands

1. Stand facing the back of a chair.

2. Loop the band across your right shoulder, bring it across your back, and loop it around your left foot.

3. Stand en pointe on your right foot. This is where you stand on the tip of your toes.

4. Reach to touch the floor with your right hand with the band is still around your right shoulder.

5. Hold for ten seconds. Relax on concentrate on the muscles you are stretching.

6. Resume a standing position.

7. Repeat two times.

8. Repeat on the opposite side.

Back Leg Lift

1. Place the band around your right shoulder and left foot.

2. Stand on your right foot.

3. Bring your left leg out to the side and back.

4. Keep your arms in the fifth arm position. Raise both arms over your head forming an oval, with your hands almost touching.

5. Hold for ten seconds while concentrating on your breathing and the muscles you are stretching.

6. Return to standing position.

7. Repeat two times.

8. Repeat on the opposite side.

Standing Quadriceps Stretch

1. The next stretch can be done using a wall, a chair, or anything stable. Loop the band around the top of your right foot then over your right shoulder and hold it in your left hand.

2. Bend your right leg up at the knee and slightly apply tension to the strap. With your left leg straight and planted on the ground, rest your right hand on the wall.

3. Turn your neck to the left so it stretches slightly.

4. Hold the pose for twenty to thirty seconds while concentrating on your breathing and the muscles you are stretching.

5. Relax for twenty seconds. Repeat two times.

Balancing Standing Quadriceps Stretch

1. Get into the quadriceps stretch position.

2. Push off the wall.

3. Hold for twenty second. Relax and concentrate on the muscles you are stretching.

4. Repeat two times.

5. Repeat for the opposite side.

LOWER BACK STRETCHES

Stretch Band Leg Press from Ground

1. Lie flat on the floor with the middle of the band behind your back at the arch and the ends looped twice around your left foot. Your right leg should be straight.

2. Push your left leg up and hold on to the band with one hand on each side.

3. Hold the pose for twenty to thirty seconds while concentrating on your breathing and the muscles you are stretching.

4. Relax for twenty seconds. Repeat two times.

5. Repeat for the opposite leg.

Lower Back Stretch Toes Pointed

1. Lay on the floor with your legs straight down. Wrap the band around your right foot.

2. Extend your right leg up in the air. Slowly, straighten your right leg.

3. Point your toe once you reach your ultimate stretch. You can also pull toward your chest for an added stretch.

4. Hold the pose for twenty to thirty seconds while concentrating on your breathing and the muscles you are stretching.

5. Relax for twenty seconds. Repeat two times.

6. Repeat on the opposite side.

Stretch Band Leg Press for Strength

1. Sit on the floor with your back straight and shoulders aligned.

2. Wrap the band around your back about mid-back

3. Loop both ends around the middle of your left foot. Place your right leg on the floor with your knee bent. Your right foot should be under your left thigh.

4. Slowly extend your left leg. Your palms should be on the floor behind your buttocks with your fingers pointing toward your body.

5. Hold the pose for twenty to thirty seconds. Relax and concentrate on the muscles you are stretching.

6. Relax for twenty seconds. Repeat two times.

7. Repeat on the opposite side.

Stretching the Core

Flex your arch.

It's important for the arch of your back to undergo some serious stretching because of all things, you don't want your back to be whacked out of alignment.

1. Lay on the floor on your stomach.

2. Wrap one end of the stretch band around both feet so it comes up between your feet.

3. Grab the other end with your hands.

4. Stretch your upper body upward and back as you lift your feet and lower legs upward.

5. Hold the band with enough tension to give a nice stretch.

6. Hold ten seconds. Relax and concentrate on the muscles you are stretching.

7. Go back to your original position, lying flat on the floor on your stomach.

8. Repeat two times.

Bonus Chapter 10

The Leg Stretcher Stretches

This chapter is an excerpt from out book *Stretching Your Limts II*. After warming up you can begin the leg stretcher exercises. If this is your only workout of the day, you can jump right in. If you are going to work out in your sport then this should be done after the workout.

The reason as stated earlier in the book, is static stretching is reserved for after the workout. Actually doing it before the workout can lead to more injuries. There is scientific evidence showing this, but covering that science is beyond the scope of this book

IT BAND KNEE FLEX

Muscles Targeted: IT band, glutes, adductors

1. Stand with your back against the door.

2. Put the strap around your right ankle.

3. Pull down gently until your foot is almost hip level.

4. Hold for 15 seconds.

5. Repeat on the opposite side.

IT BAND KNEE FLEX WITH CALF RAISE

Muscles Targeted: IT band, glutes, adductors, calf of supporting leg

1. Stand with your back against the door.

2. Put the strap around your right ankle.

3. Pull down gently until your foot is almost hip level.

4. Raise your left heel off the ground.

5. Hold for 15 seconds.

6. Repeat on the opposite side.

BACK LEG FLEX PULL

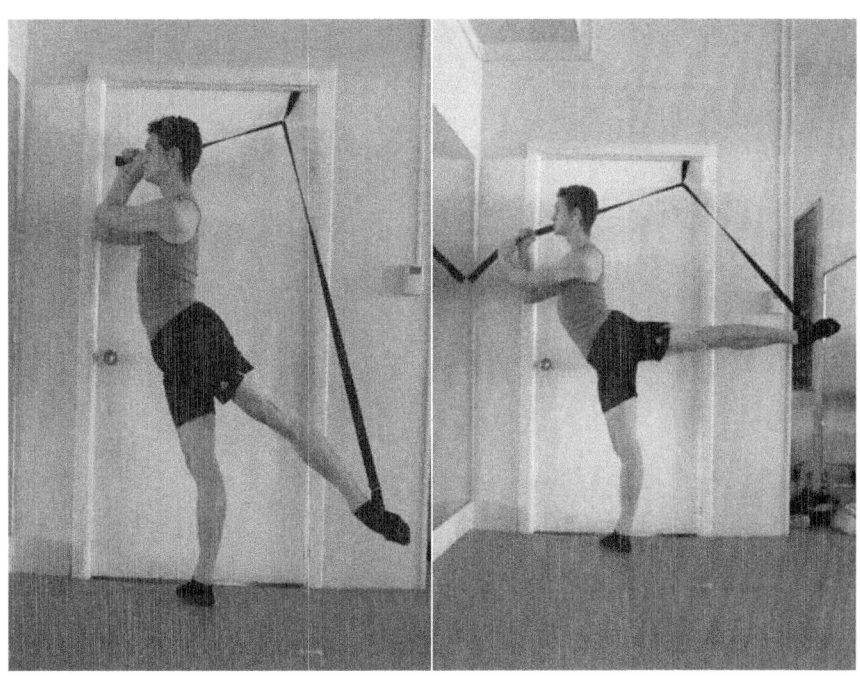

Muscles Targeted: Quadriceps and calves of supporting leg, hamstrings and adductors.

1. Stand straight and tall, facing sideways.

2. Loop the ankle of your back leg into the leg stretcher.

3. Rotate slowly to where your hip is out externally.

4. Keep your extended leg straight.

5. Pull down gently on the strap with your palms and wrists facing your body.

6. Repeat on other side.

BACK LEG FLEX PULL WITH CALF LIFT

Muscles Targeted: Quadriceps of supporting leg, hamstrings and adductors for lifting leg, hips, calves

1. Stand straight and tall, facing sideways.

2. Loop the ankle of your back leg into the leg stretcher.

3. Rotate slowly to where your hip is out externally.

4. Keep your extended leg straight.

5. Pull down gently on the strap with your palms and wrists facing your body.

6. Raise your heel off the ground and hold for 5 seconds.

BOW STRETCH

Muscles Targeted: quadriceps on supporting leg, back, hips

1. Stand straight and tall, facing sideways.

2. Loop the ankle of your back leg into the leg stretcher.

3. Rotate slowly to where your hip is out externally.

4. Keep your extended leg bent.

5. Pull down gently on the strap with your palms and wrist facing inward.

6. Repeat with the other leg.

BOW STRETCH WITH HEEL RAISE

Muscles Targeted: quadriceps and calf on supporting leg, back, hips

1. Stand straight and tall, facing sideways.

2. Loop the ankle of your back leg into the leg stretcher.

3. Rotate slowly to where your hip is out externally.

4. Keep your extended leg bent.

5. Pull down gently on the strap with your palms and wrist facing inward.

6. Raise your heel off the floor as you exhale by contracting the calves. Hold the top contraction for 15 seconds.

7. Repeat with the other leg.

SIDE LEG PULL

Muscles Targeted: Adductor muscles

1. Stand straight and tall with your back to the door.

2. Put your foot through the loop and then pull your leg out to the side.

3. Pull the strap down gently,

4. Keep your hips aligned and your leg straight.

5. Work the opposite side.

SIDE LEG PULL WITH BALANCE

Muscles Targeted: Adductor muscles

1. Stand straight and tall with your back to the door.

2. Put your foot through the loop and then pull your leg out to the side.

3. Pull the strap down gently and bring the arm above the head as pictured.

4. Keep your hips aligned and your leg straight.

5. Work the opposite side.

SIDE LEG PULL WITH SPLITS

Muscles Targeted: Adductor muscles

1. Stand straight and tall with your back to the door.

2. Put your foot through the loop and then pull your leg out to the side.

3. Pull the strap down gently until you are in a full split. Go very slowly and focus on your balance.

4. Keep your hips aligned and your leg straight.

5. Work the opposite side.

ADVANCED SIDE LEG PULL WITH BALANCE

Muscles Targeted: Adductor muscles

1. Stand straight and tall with your back to the door.

2. Put your foot through the loop and then pull your leg out to the side as you bend at the waist with hips facing forward.

3. Pull the strap down gently, and bring your arm out carefully balancing.

4. Keep your hips aligned and your leg straight.

5. Work the opposite side.

SIDE PULL-CALF RAISE

Muscles Targeted: Adductor of lifting leg, calf of supporting leg

1. Stand straight and tall with your back to the door.

2. Put your foot through the loop and then pull your leg out to the side.

3. Pull the strap down gently

4. Keep your hips aligned and your leg straight.

5. Lift the heel of the foot on the ground up as you pull your other leg up.

6. Work the opposite side.

TOP LEG STRETCH SHOULDERS OUTWARD

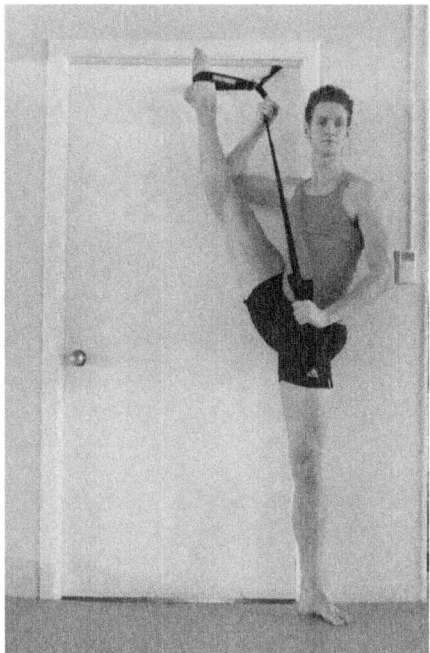

Muscles Targeted: Hamstrings, adductors

1. Stand straight and tall, facing the door.

2. With one foot flat, toes pointing to the door, loop the other foot through the band.

3. Hold the strap with bended elbows, holding it close to your body.

4. Gently pull your leg up with toes pointed.

5. Rotate your shoulders and hips slightly towards your extended leg.

6. Hold 10 seconds.

7. Work the opposite side.

TOP LEG STRETCH SHOULDERS SQUARED

Muscles Targeted: Hamstrings, adductors

1. Stand straight and tall, facing the door.

2. With one foot flat, toes pointing to the door, loop the other foot through the band.

3. Hold the strap with bended elbows, holding it close to your body and hips facing forward.

4. Gently pull your leg up with toes pointed.

5. Hold 10 seconds.

6. Work the opposite side.

CHAIR LIFT

Muscles Targeted: Hamstrings

1. Sit straight up in a chair.

2. Loop one leg through the leg stretcher band.

3. Place the other leg down with pointed toes and leg slightly bent.

4. Slowly and gently pull your leg up.

5. Hold 10 seconds

6. Repeat on the other side.

UP AGAINST THE WALL

Muscles Targeted: Adductors

1. Stand straight with your face to the wall.

2. Loop one ankle into the strap.

3. Plant one foot on the floor, angled outward.

4. Slowly pull the strap to extend your opposite leg up.

5. Hold for 10 seconds.

6. Repeat on opposite side.

FRONT LEG PULL

Muscles Targeted: Hamstrings

1. Stand straight and tall, facing the door.

2. With one foot flat, toes pointing to the door, loop the other foot through the band.

3. Hold the strap with bended elbows, holding it close to your body.

4. Gently pull your leg up with toes pointed.

5. Hold 10 seconds.

6. Work the opposite side.

FRONT LEG PULL INTO SPLITS

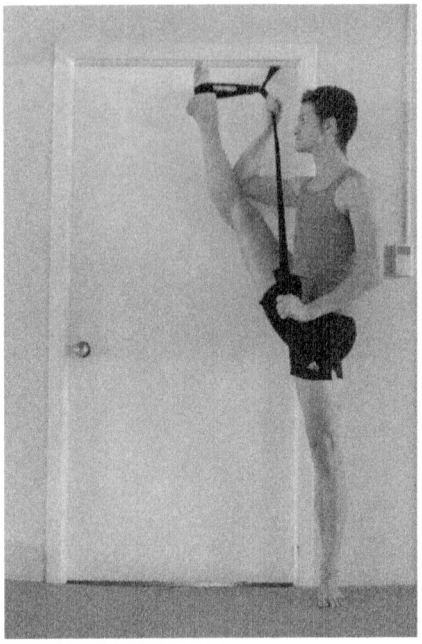

Muscles Targeted: Hamstrings

1. Stand straight and tall, parallel to the door.

2. With one foot flat, toes pointing away from the door, loop the other foot through the band.

3. Hold the strap with bended elbows, holding it close to your body.

4. Gently pull your leg up with toes pointed.

5. Pull until you reach your full extension.

6. Hold 10 seconds.

7. Work the opposite side.

FRONT LEG PULL WITH CALF STRETCH

Muscles Targeted: Hamstrings, calf

1. Stand straight and tall, facing the door.

2. With one foot flat, toes pointing away from the door, loop the other foot through the band.

3. Hold the strap with bended elbows, holding it close to your body.

4. Gently pull your leg up with toes pointed.

5. Raise the supporting heel off the ground.

6. Hold 10 seconds.

7. Work the opposite side.

GET BACK JACK

Muscles Targeted: Adductors, hamstrings, quadriceps

1. Stand facing the side.

2. Plant one foot on the ground, toes facing forward.

3. Loop the band through your other foot with toes pointed.

4. With both hands, gently pull your leg up.

5. Hold 10 seconds.

6. Work the other side.

GET BACK JACK WITH HEEL RAISE

Muscles Targeted: Adductors, hamstrings, quadriceps, calf

1. Stand facing the side.

2. Plant one foot on the ground, toes facing forward.

3. Loop the band through your other foot with toes pointed.

4. With both hands, gently pull your leg up.

5. Hold 10 seconds.

6. Work the other side.

CALF STRETCH

Muscles Targeted: Hamstrings

1. From the side hamstring stretch position place your foot in the center of the flexibility strap as shown above.

2. Gently pull your body towards your knee.

3. Hold the pose for twenty to thirty seconds while concentrating on your breathing and the muscles you are stretching.

4. Relax for a few seconds.

5. Switch and repeat on the opposite side.

KNEELING QUADRICEPS STRETCH

Muscles Targeted: Quadriceps

1. Stand with your legs a hip-width apart.

2. Loop the band around the middle of your left foot, and then bring it over your right shoulder.

3. Step forward with your right leg and plant your left knee on the floor so it is bent and your right foot is on the ground.

4. With your left hand on the floor, lower your body to where your front left thigh is parallel to the floor. At this point, the flexibility strap should be snug.

5. Hold for twenty to thirty seconds while concentrating on your breathing and the muscles you are stretching.

6. Relax.

7. Switch and repeat on the opposite side.

STANDING FRONT SPLIT

Muscles Targeted: Inner and outer thighs

1. Stand facing a chair.

2. Hold the band with your right hand, wrapping it around your wrist once.

3. Take the other end of the band over your right shoulder and loop it around your left foot.

4. Hold onto the chair with your left hand.

5. Lean forward toward the chair, slightly arching your back.

6. As you are leaning in, bring your left foot up over your head so you are basically doing the split in the air.

7. Slowly lower your left foot back to the ground while bringing your torso back to a standing position.

8. Hold for twenty to thirty seconds while concentrating on your breathing and the muscles you are stretching.

9. Repeat two times.

Switch sides and repeat.

STANDING QUADRICEPS STRETCH

Muscles Targeted: Quadriceps

1. The next stretch can be done using a wall, a chair, or anything stable. Loop the flexibility strap around the top of your right foot then over your right shoulder and hold it in your left hand.

2. Bend your right leg up at the knee and slightly apply tension to the strap. With your left leg straight and planted on the ground, rest your right hand on the wall.

3. Hold the pose for twenty to thirty seconds while concentrating on your breathing and the muscles you are stretching.

BALANCING STANDING QUADRICEPS STRETCH

Muscles Targeted: Quadriceps, balance

1. Get into the s quadriceps stretch.

2. Push off the wall.

3. Hold for twenty second. Relax and concentrate on the muscles you are stretching.

4. Repeat two times.

5. Repeat for the opposite side.

LEG PRESS FROM GROUND

Muscles Targeted: Lower Back, Hamstring

1. Lie flat on the floor with the middle of the band behind your back at the arch and the ends looped twice around your left foot. Your right leg should be straight.

2. Push your left leg up and hold on to the band with one hand on each side.

3. Hold the pose for twenty to thirty seconds while concentrating on your breathing and the muscles you are stretching.

4. Relax for twenty seconds. Repeat two times.

Gymnastics Strength Band is a fantastic piece of equipment to better your flexibility, balance and strength. It can be a bit hard to adapt too, but the gains are well worth it.

Remember, Gymnastics Strength Band works on strength training and should not be used every day. Tools that can be used every day are the Ballet Stretch Bands, or the Leg Stretcher door strap.

We have instructional books for both of these fantastic items that utilize static stretching. They are different exercises than those which are found in Gymnastics Strength Band book.

We wish you the best of luck on your flexibility as you stretch your way to the top!

When you are cooling down it is great to rehydrate and also after exercise. Here is an excerpt from our book that is fantastic for post-exercise drinks.

Chapter 11

Cooling Down

Cooling down is every bit as important as warming up, and this is actually when you can get some good stretch gains.

Why Is Stretching After a Workout Important?

There is some science to back up cooling down. For athletes, this isn't usually a high priority, but there are many reasons why you should cool down. This is also a great debriefing time for a team or for you as an individual. Meditation, goal setting and unwinding can be accompanied into this cool down.

- It helps you recover.

- Your core body temperature lowers at a slow and safe rate.

- Your blood pressure can decrease safely.

- The build-up of lactic acid within your muscles is allowed to release.

- The adrenaline you have accumulated is able to decrease from the "fight or flight" mode.

- This is also the time you gain the most flexibility.

- This is the most important time for static stretching.

Things to Consider When Cooling Down

- **Take slow deep breaths**

As you know by now, your body works harder at everything when it is in exercise mode. Your lungs, your heart, even your circulation is going over and above to provide your body with what it needs for the workout.

During the actual time you are using the energy, like while you are dancing, this is a great setup. But, once the routine is over, your body is a bit confused. It is still desperately seeking to find a way to deliver all the extra blood and oxygen to fuel your needs but...your engine is turned off. Cooling down by slowing your breathing allows your body to change modes from a rapid heart rate to a slower, more suitable one and to do so smoothly and without chaos.

- **Move slowly and deliberately**

Gradually transition from your strenuous workout to your cool down so it will be a gentle process. You certainly don't want to send your body into shock by alarming it. If you go from full exertion to none at all, you can imagine the mixed messages your brain is sending to your muscles, organs, etc. Simply decrease your activity, little by little, by properly cooling down through a method such as static stretching.

- **Hydrate**

In your cool down, be sure to drink up. Dehydration can lead to a myriad of symptoms. Adding hydration to your cool down helps to eliminate the chance of that happening. It will also refill you with energy and reduce soreness and cramping too.

- **Ease into stretches**

Remember the noodle. Warm muscles will stretch further. During your cool down is the perfect time to add in some static stretches to extend your muscles and increase your flexibility. This is actually where you get most of your flexibility gains.

Cool Factors of a Cool Down Done Correctly

- Hold pose 30 seconds or longer

- Move slowly and gently

- Unwind

- Rehydrate

Using your Gymnastics Stretch Band

You would not use your Gymnastics Stretch Band during a cool down. It is for building strength. You could, however, use Ballet Bands or the stunt strap which we go over in our first two books Stretching Your Limits and Stretching Your Limits 2.

Cool-Downs

Although you can certainly cool all your muscles down, be certain to cool down those that you used. Your muscles have heated up so they physically need to cool down.

A great way to cool down is to repeat some of the movements you did during your strenuous workout but do them slower and gentler. This does not include Gymnastics Strength Band. Do not include those.

Chapter 11

Cool Down Exercises

Cool Roll

It's time to roll it up. Calm your body back into a relaxed state with this cool down.

1. Stand with your arms beside your body.

2. Roll your neck with your chin to your chest.

3. Roll your back all the way down.

4. Touch your hands to the floor.

5. Roll with your back all the way back up.

6. Repeat ten times.

Roll t Up

It's time to roll it up, literally. As you begin to calm your body from its hard work back to a normally functioning zone, the same rolling exercises you used to get warmed up are perfect for cooling down as well.

1. Stand with your arms beside your body.

2. Roll your neck with your chin to your chest.

3. Roll your back all the way down, touching your hands to the floor.

4. Now, roll with your back all the way back up.

5. Repeat ten times.

Side Swipe

If you've ever gotten a cramp in your side, you will appreciate the importance of this cool-down exercise.

Remember, your circulation is greatly slowed to your digestive area during your workout, and afterwards, the blood attempts to flow there again. So, help it along its way with this must-do exercise.

1. Stand with your feet about shoulders' width apart.

2. Raise your right hand above your head and reach to the side as you stretch to the left.

3. Slightly roll your back around and come back to the above stance.

4. Press down to the left to increase your side stretch.

5. Hold for ten seconds and come up to your original position.

6. Repeat ten times on the other side.

Back Thigh Stretch

Chances are, the workout or routine has placed a pretty good strain on your thighs. You have elongated them, so now it's time to get them back to their comfort zone.

1. With your feet in a wide stance, turned to the side with toe to heel, turn your body to face the side, toes pointing forward.

2. Roll forward with your back, touching your hands to the ground or, if that is too intense, touch your shin instead.

3. Stretch your back and the back of your legs.

4. Hold for twenty to thirty seconds while you breathe deeply and relax the back of your thighs.

5. Return to side stance position.

6. Repeat five to ten times.

7. Repeat on the other side.

Chapter 12

Putting it all Together

You have seen three different stretching tools now how do you use them in a routine?

The formula is actually pretty simple. You can use the Leg Stretcher and the Ballet Stretch band every day. It is great to use after practice. Do not use it before practice, as you need to use dynamic stretching before a practice.

Step 1: Warm up with dynamic stretching. Choose from the warm up exercises. Do about 5-10 minutes of these exercises.

Step 2: Use the Gymnastics Strengthening Stretches 2-3 times per week.

- Option 1: Choose 1-2 exercises from each muscle group

- Option 2: Do upper body stretches one day and lower body stretches the next. If you chose this option, only work out every other day. If you do the entire body take a day off in between.

Step 3: Finish up with 5-10 stretches with the Ballet Stretch Band or the Leg Stretcher, or static stretching with no equipment. Target each body part. This final stage really helps but be sure to do this after a workout.

If you are going to class and then want to add more stretching begin with Step 2. However, if you are doing strength training in class, be sure and do the Gymnastics Strength training on the same day, so your body has time to rest. For a young body, you could also use step 2 as stand alone stretching, in the off season and skip to Step 3.

Important Tips:

- Cool down with passive stretching.

- Train with the Gymnastics Strength Bands every other day or twice a week, but do not train two days in a row.

- Rest for 24 hours between stretching bouts.

Use the stretch bands and the leg stretcher daily if you would like. Use them after practice. They are not good to ue before practice.

The Gymnastics Strength Band should only be used 2-3 times per week. It should also only be used every other day. The reason being you are training strength. You must have a day of rest after strength training. When you train strength, you tear your muscles down. It takes time to repair. You need the day of rest to repair and grow stronger.

Conclusion

Training in gymnastics is such a great endeavor as one works on the body, mental toughness and strength. Adding strength and flexibility can help you rise to your personal best with flexibility. We wish you the best on your journey. Keep stretching your limits. It is a long way to the top but you can get there!

Printed in Great Britain
by Amazon

15790657R00098

The North Sea

**A Highway of Economic and Cultural Exchange
Character – History**

Editors:
Arne Bang-Andersen
Basil Greenhill
Egil Harald Grude

Norwegian University Press
Stavanger – Oslo – Bergen – Tromsø